All the Best Songs of Praise & Worship 3

More Contemporary Favorites

PUBLISHING COMPANY

www.lillenas.com

1

How Great Is Our God *

Psalm 104:1-2

C. T., J. R. and E. C.

CHRIS TOMLIN, JESSE REEVE
and ED CASH

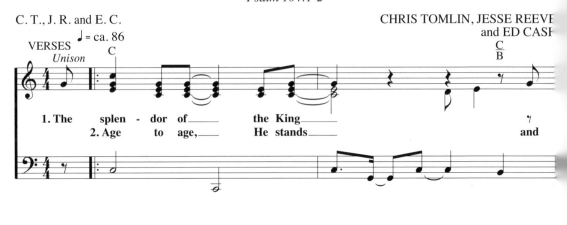

1. The splen - dor of_____ the King_____
2. Age to age,_____ He stands_____ and

clothed in maj - es - ty,_____ Let all the earth_ re - joice,_____
time is in_____ His hands,_____ Be - gin - ning and_ the End,_____

_____ let all the earth_ re - joice._____ He wraps
_____ Be - gin - ning and_ the End._____ The God -

_____ Him - self_____ in light_____ and
- head, three_____ in one,_____

heart will sing___ how great___ is our God!___

great, how great___ is our God!___

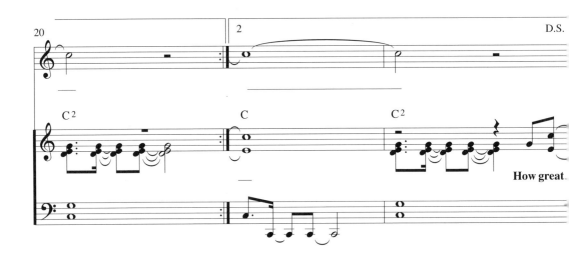

How great___

Blessed Be Your Name*

Nehemiah 9:5

B. R. and M. R.

BETH REDMAN
and MATT REDMAN

VERSES ♩ = ca. 120

1. Bless - ed be____ Your name____ in the land that____ is plen -
2. Bless - ed be____ Your name____ when the sun's shin - ing down____

- ti - ful;____ Where the streams of____ a - bun - dance flow,____ bless-
____ on me;____ When the world's all____ as it____ should be,____ bless-

ed be Your name;____ Bless - ed be____
ed be Your name;____ Bless - ed be____

____ Your name____ when I'm found in____ the des - ert place,____ When I
____ Your name____ on the road marked with suf - fer - ing;____ Tho' there's

*This song is included on the Volume 2 companion recording.

3

Here I Am to Worship*

Psalm 95:6

T. H.

TIM HUGHES

1. Light of the world, You stepped down in-to dark - ness,
2. King of all days, O so high - ly ex - alt - ed,

O - pened my eyes, let me see
Glo - rious in heav - en a - bove,

Beau - ty that made this heart a - dore You,
Hum - bly You came to the earth You cre - a - ted,

Hope of a life spent with You.
All for love's sake be - came poor.

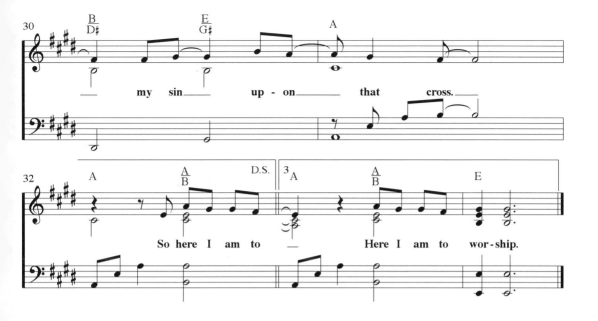

You Are My King*   4

B. F.   ♩ = ca. 70

BILLY FOOTE

*This song is included on the companion recording. Intro on recording is 1 measure.

5

Forever*

Psalm 136

C.T.

CHRIS TOMLIN

1. Give thanks to the Lord___ our God and___ King;___ His
(2.) might - y hand___ and out - stretched arm;___ His
(3.) ris - ing to___ the set - ting___ sun___

love en - dures___ for-ev - er. For He is good,_ He is a -
And by the grace of God___ For the life___ that's

bove all___ things;_ His love en - dures___ for-ev - er. Sing
been re - born;_
car - ry___ on;_

In the Presence of Jehovah

Psalm 73:23-28

6

G. D. and B. D.

GERON DAVIS and
BECKY DAVIS

7

Shout to the Lord*

D. Z.

♩ = ca. 80

DARLENE ZSCHECH

Shout to the Lord,— all the earth,— let us sing— Pow-er and maj-

-es-ty, praise— to the King;— Moun-tains bow down— and the seas—

— will roar— at the sound— of Your name.—

I sing for joy— at the work— of Your hands,— For-ev-er I'll love

2nd time to Coda

— You, for-ev-er I'll stand;— Noth-ing com-pares— to the prom-

*This song is included on the companion recording and starts with the verse. Intro on recording is 2 measures.

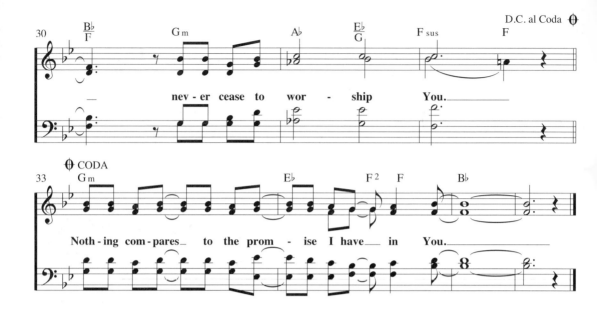

D.C. al Coda

nev - er cease to wor - ship You._____

CODA

Noth-ing com-pares___ to the prom - ise I have___ in You._____

8   Come, Now Is the Time to Worship*

B. D.

BRIAN DOERKSEN

♩ = ca. 98

Unison

Come,   now is the time___ to wor - ship.___

Come,   now is the time__ to give___ your heart.

Come,   just as you are___ to wor - ship.___

9

Amazing Grace*
(My Chains Are Gone)

JOHN NEWTON, JOHN P. REES,
CHRIS TOMLIN and LOUIE GIGLIO

Virginia Harmony, 1831, CHRIS TOMLIN
and LOUIE GIGLIO

1. A - maz - ing grace how sweet the sound that
(2. 'Twas) grace that taught my heart to fear, and

saved a wretch like me. I once was lost, but
grace my fears re - lieved. How pre - cious did that

now I'm found, was blind but now I see. 2. 'Twas
grace ap - pear the hour I first be

lieved. My chains are gone, I've been set free. My God, my

3

Here I Am to Worship*

Psalm 95:6

T. H.

TIM HUGHES

VERSES

♩ = ca. 74

Unison

1. Light of the world, You stepped down in - to dark - ness,
2. King of all days, O so high - ly ex - alt - ed,

O - pened my eyes, let me see
Glo - rious in heav - en a - bove,

Beau - ty that made this heart a - dore You,
Hum - bly You came to the earth You cre - a - ted,

Hope of a life spent with You.
All for love's sake be - came poor.

You Are My King*

4

BILLY FOOTE

*This song is included on the companion recording. Intro on recording is 1 measure.

5

Forever*

Psalm 136

C. T.

CHRIS TOMLIN

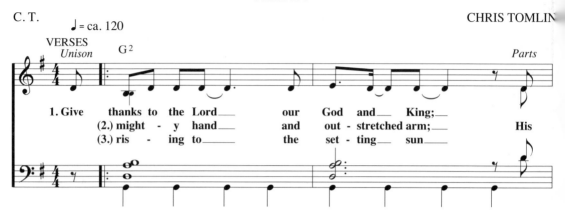

*This song is included on the Volume 2 companion recording.

In the Presence of Jehovah

Psalm 73:23-28

6

G. D. and B. D.

GERON DAVIS and
BECKY DAVIS

7 Shout to the Lord*

D. Z.

DARLENE ZSCHECH

♩ = ca. 80

2nd time to Coda

*This song is included on the companion recording and starts with the verse. Intro on recording is 2 measures.

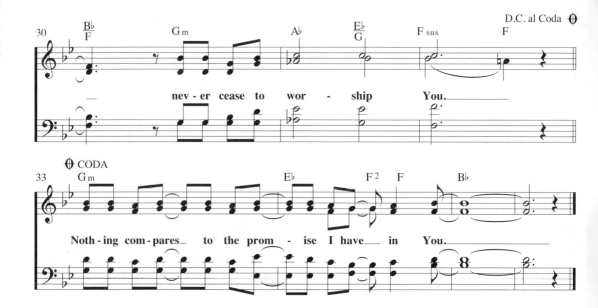

D.C. al Coda

8

Come, Now Is the Time to Worship*

B. D.

BRIAN DOERKSEN

Come, now is the time___ to wor - ship.___

Come, now is the time___ to give___ your heart.

Come, just as you are___ to wor - ship.___

9

Amazing Grace*
(My Chains Are Gone)

JOHN NEWTON, JOHN P. REES,
CHRIS TOMLIN and LOUIE GIGLIO

Virginia Harmony, 1831, CHRIS TOMLIN
and LOUIE GIGLIO

*This song is included on the companion recording. Intro on recording is 4 measures.

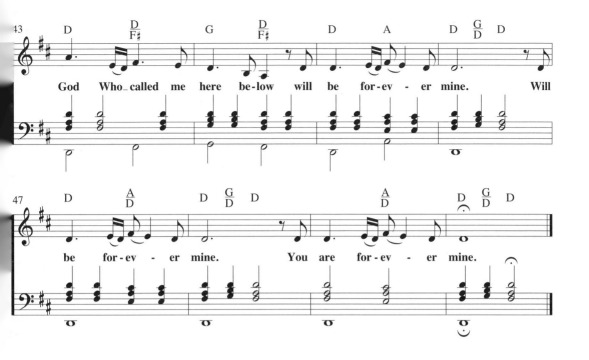

Everlasting God*

B. B. and K. R.

BRENTON BROWN
and KEN RILEY

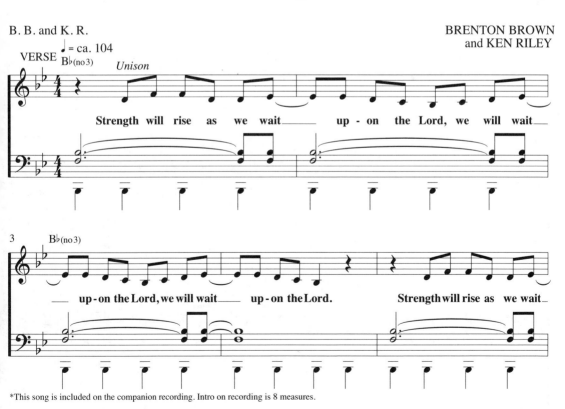

*This song is included on the companion recording. Intro on recording is 8 measures.

up-on the Lord, we will wait up-on the Lord, we will wait up-on the Lord. Our God,

You reign for - ev - er. Our Hope,

our Strong De - li - ver - er!

CHORUS

You are the Ev - er - last - ing God, the Ev -

er - last - ing God. You do not faint, You

11   The Heart of Worship*

M. R.

MATT REDMAN

*This song is included on the companion recording. Intro on recording is 2 measures.

I'm sor-ry, Lord, for the thing__ I've made__ it, When it's all a-bout You;__ all a-bout You,__ Je - sus.

12 Who Am I?*

M. H.

MARK HALL

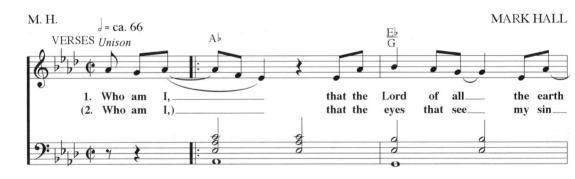

1. Who am I,__ that the Lord of all__ the earth
(2. Who am I,) that the eyes that see__ my sin

would care to know__ my name,__ would
would look on me__ with love__ and

13   Beautiful One*

Psalm 18:1

T. H.

TIM HUGHES

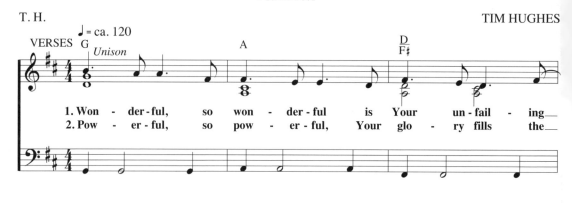

1. Won - der-ful, so won - der-ful is Your un - fail - ing love,
2. Pow - er-ful, so pow - er-ful, Your glo - ry fills the skies,

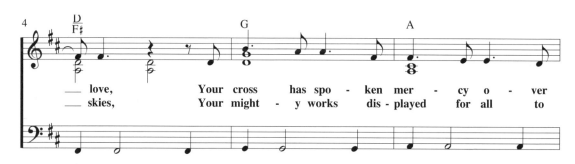

Your cross has spo - ken mer - cy o - ver me.
Your might - y works dis - played for all to see.

No eye has seen, no
The beau - ty of Your

ear has heard, no heart could ful - ly know How
maj - es - ty a - wakes my heart to sing: How

*This song is included on the Volume 2 companion recording.

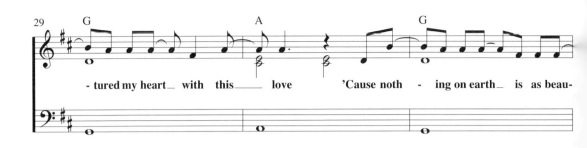

-tured my heart_ with this_____ love   'Cause noth - ing on earth_ is as beau-

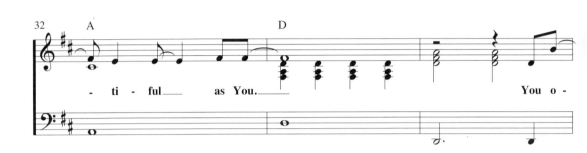

- ti - ful_____ as You._____   You o -

- pened my eyes_____ to Your won - ders a - new,_____ You cap -

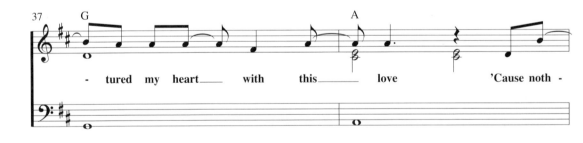

- tured my heart_____ with this_____ love   'Cause noth -

- ing on earth_ is as beau - ti - ful_____ as You._____

14

Thank You, Lord

Psalm 30:11-12

D. J.

DENNIS JERNIGAN

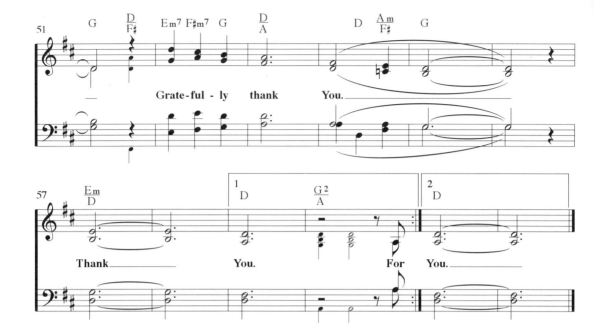

15

In Christ Alone*

1 Corinthians 3:11

K. G. and S. T.

KEITH GETTY and
STUART TOWNEND

1. In Christ a - lone my hope is found, He is my
2. In Christ a - lone– who took on flesh, Full - ness of
3. There in the ground His bod - y lay, Light of the
4. No guilt in life, no fear in death, This is the

light, my strength, my song; This cor - ner - stone, this
God in help - less babe. This gift of love and
world by dark - ness slain; Then burst - ing forth in
pow'r of Christ in me; From life's first cry to

*This song is included on the Volume 2 companion recording.

16
All in the Name of Jesus

Acts 4:12; Colossians 2:9-10

S. R. A.

STEPHEN R. ADAMS

17 You Are My All in All*

D. J.

DENNIS JERNIGAN

1. You are my strength when I am weak; You are the trea-sure that I
2. Tak-ing my sin, my cross, my shame; Ris-ing a-gain, I bless Your

seek. You are my all in all.
name. You are my all in all.

Seek-ing You as a pre-cious jewel; Lord, to give up, I'd be a
When I fall down You pick me up; When I am dry you fill my

fool. You are my all in all.
cup. You are my all in all.

CHORUS

Je - sus, Lamb of God, Wor - thy is Your name.

*This song is included on the companion recording. Intro on recording is 4 measures.

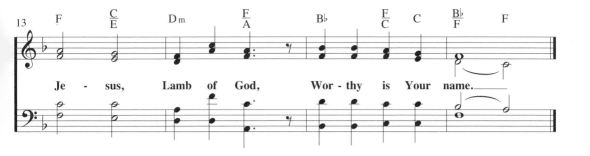

13

F | C/E | Dm | F/A | B♭ | F/C | C | B♭/F | F

Je - sus, Lamb of God, Wor - thy is Your name.___

Hungry*

(Falling On My Knees)

Psalm 42:1-2

KATHRYN SCOTT

K. S.   ♩ = ca. 86

VERSES
Unison   D | Bm7 | D/A

1. Hun-gry, I___ come to You, for___ I know You sat - is -
2. Bro-ken, I___ run to You, for___ Your arms are o - pen

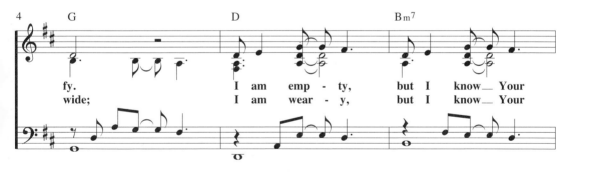

4   G | D | Bm7

fy.   I am emp - ty,   but I know___ Your
wide;   I am wear - y,   but I know___ Your

7   D/A | G | 2-part A

love does not___ run dry.   So I wait for
touch re - stores___ my life.

*The track has 2 additional measures in ending 1.

Worthy Is the Lamb*

Revelation 5:11-14

D. Z.

DARLENE ZSCHECH

20

Mighty to Save*

B. F. and R. M.

BEN FIELDING and
REUBEN MORGAN

1. ⅞ Ev-'ry-one needs com-pas - sion,　　love that's nev - er fail-
2. So take_ me　as You find_ me,　　all　my fears and fail-

- ing,　　Let mer - cy　fall on_ me._　　⅞ Ev-'ry-one needs for-give-
- ures,　⅞ Fill my　life a - gain._　　I give_ my life　to fol -

- ness,　　the kind - ness　of　a　Sav　-　ior,_　　The
- low,　⅞ ev'-ry-thing　I　be - lieve_　in,_　　Now

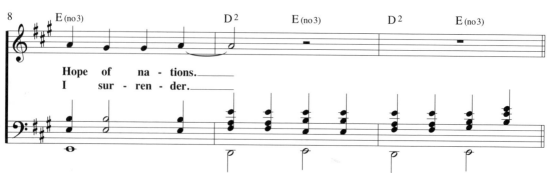

Hope　of　na - tions._
I　sur - ren - der._

might - y to save,___ He is might - y to save.___ For -
ev - er, Au - thor of Sal - va - tion, He rose and
con - quered the grave,___ Je - sus con - quered the grave.___

Indescribable*

21

Psalm 104

LAURA STORY and
JESSE REEVES

LAURA STORY

♩. = ca. 60

VERSES Em   *Unison*

1. From the high - est of heights to the depths of the___
2. Who has told ev - 'ry light - ning bolt where it should___

*This song is included on the Volume 2 companion recording.

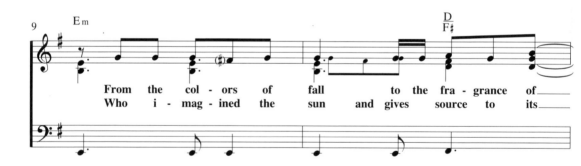

M. H.

MATT MAHER

1. Great is__ Your faith - ful - ness,__ O God.____

You wres - tle with____ the sin - ner's heart.____

You lead__ us by____ still wa - ters in - to mer - cy,

And noth - ing can____ keep us__ a - part.____ So re -

mem - ber__ Your peo - ple, Re - mem - ber__ Your chil - dren. Re -

*This song is included on the companion recording. Intro on recording is 4 measures.

23 Sing to the King*

B. F. and C. S. H.

BILLY FOOTE an
CHARLES SILVESTER HORN

VERSES *Opt. harmony 2nd time*
♩ = ca. 125

1. Sing to the King who is coming to reign.
2. For His returning we watch and we pray.

Glory to Jesus, the Lamb that was slain.
We will be ready, the dawn of that day.

Life and salvation His empire shall bring,
We'll join in singing with all the redeeme

And joy to the nations when Jesus is King
'Cause Satan in vanqished and Jesus is King

*This song is included on the companion recording. Intro on recording is 4 measures.

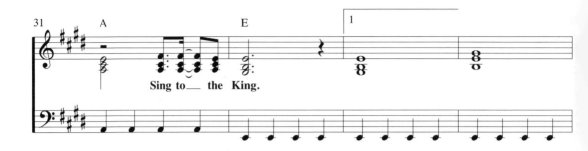

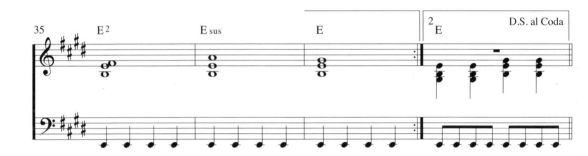

24   Hallelujah (Your Love Is Amazing)*

Romans 8:35-39

B. B. and B. D.

BRENTON BROWN and
BRIAN DOERKSEN

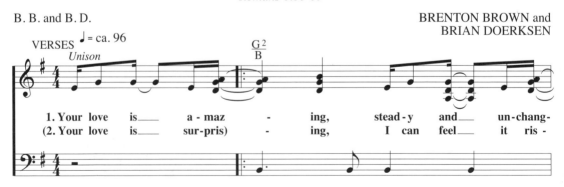

1. Your love is___ a - maz - ing, stead - y and___ un-chang-
(2. Your love is___ sur-pris) - ing, I can feel___ it ris -

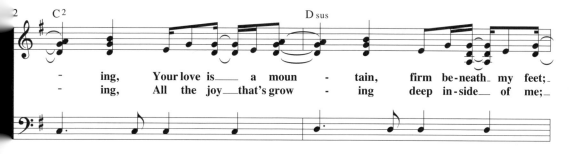

ing,   Your love is____ a moun - tain,   firm be-neath_ my feet;_

ing,   All the joy___that's grow - ing   deep in-side_ of me;_

Your love is____ a mys - t'ry,   how You gen - tly lift____

Ev - 'ry time_ I see_____ you,   all Your good - ness shines_

me   When I am_ sur-round - ed,   Your love car - ries me.

through,   I can feel_ this God_____ song,   ris - ing up_ in me.

CHORUS

Hal - le - lu - jah,   Hal - le - lu -

25

My Redeemer Lives*

Job 19:25-27

R. M.

REUBEN MORGAN

*This song is included on the companion recording. Intro on recording is 8 measures.

*Measure 17-20 may be deleted on 2nd and 3rd pass. But the vocal notes "My Re-" need to be sung at the end of measure 16.

*Optional Chorus Repeat, after playing measure 43 repeat back to measure 17 but the vocal notes "My Re-" need to be sung at the end of measure 16.

Hosanna *

26

PAUL BALOCHE and
BRENTON BROWN

*This song is included on the companion recording. Intro on recording is 4 measures.

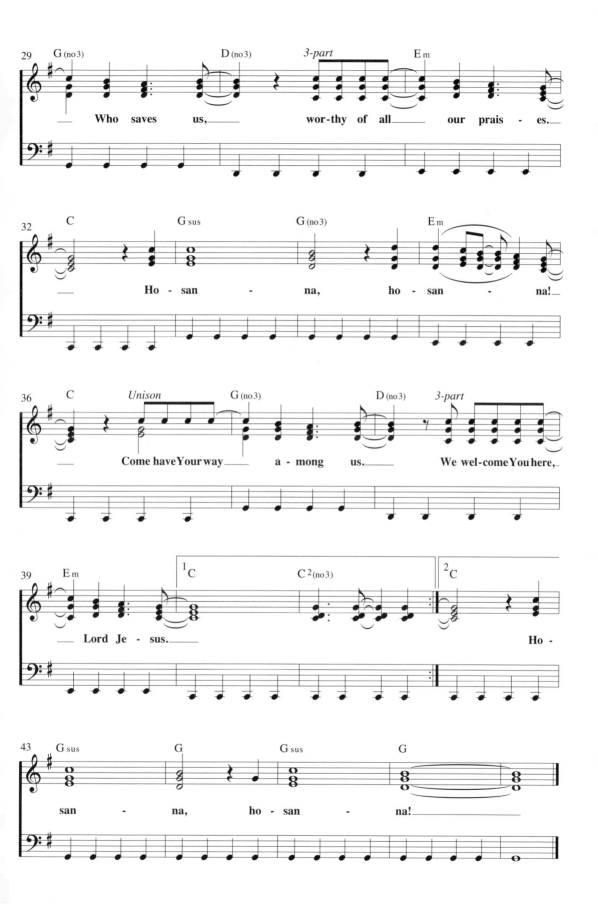

27 I Am Free*

28

He Knows My Name*

*This song is included on the companion recording. Intro on recording is 4 measures.

hears me when I call. hears me when I call. He

hears me when I call. He hears me when I call.

29   How Deep the Father's Love for Us*

1 John 4:10

S. T.

♩ = ca. 108

STUART TOWNEND

1. How deep the Fa - ther's love for us, how
2. Be - hold the man up - on a cross, my
3. I will not boast in an - y - thing, no

vast be - yond all mea - sure, That He should give
sin up - on His shoul - ders; A - shamed, I hear
gifts, no pow'r, no wis - dom; But I will boast

30 Take My Life*

S. U.

SCOTT UNDERWOOD

*This song is included on the companion recording. Intro on recording is 2 measures. Verse 4 not on recording.

*On the recording, optional loop last time measure 20-27.

31   Your Name*

P. B. and G. P.

PAUL BALOCHE and
GLENN PACKIAM

You Shine

Psalm 118:6; Isaiah 60:1

BRIAN DOERKSON

Why should I fear man when You made the heavens? Why should I be afraid when You put the stars in place? Why should I lose heart when I know how great You are?

33

Once Again

Galatians 6:14; Philippians 2:5-11

M. R.

MATT REDMA

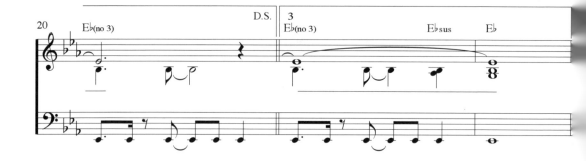

34

The Wonderful Cross*

ISAAC WATTS, CHRIS TOMLIN,
JESSE REEVES and J. D. WALT

LOWELL MASON, CHRIS TOMLIN,
JESSE REEVES and J. D. WALT

1. When I sur - vey the won - drous
2. See, from His head, His

cross On which the Prince of
feet, Sor - row and love flow

Glo - ry died, My rich - est
min - gled down. Did e'er such

*This song is included on the companion recording. Intro on recording is 4 measures.

35

Offering*

Hebrews 13:15

PAUL BALOCHE

P. B. ♩ = ca. 66

The sun— can-not com-pare— to the glo-ry of— Your love;

There is— no shad-ow in— Your pres-ence;—

No mor - tal man would dare— to stand— be-fore— Your throne.

Be-fore— the Ho - ly One— of Heav-en;— It's

on - ly by— Your blood and it's on - ly thro'— Your mer - cy,

36

All Who Are Thirsty

Isaiah 55:1

B. B. and G. R.

BRENTON BROWN an
GLENN ROBERTSO[...]

All who are thirst - y, _____ all who are _____ weak, _____ come to the foun - tain; _____ Dip your heart in the stream of life. Let the pain and the sor - row _____ be washed a - way _____ In the waves of His mer - cy _____ as deep cries

37 Be unto Your Name

Psalm 90:1-6; Revelation 4:8; 5:13

L. D. and G. S.

LYNN DESHAZ[O]
and GARY SADLE[R]

1. We are a mo - ment, You are for - ev - er,
2. We are the bro - ken, You are the heal - er,

Lord of the a - ges, God be - fore time;
Je - sus, Re - deem - er, might - y to save;

We are a va - por, You are e - ter - nal,
You are the love song we'll sing for - ev - er,

Love ev - er - last - ing, reign - ing on high.
Bow - ing be - fore You, bless - ing Your name.

38

How Can I Keep from Singing?*

C. T., E. C. and M. R.

CHRIS TOMLIN, ED CASH
and MATT REDMAN

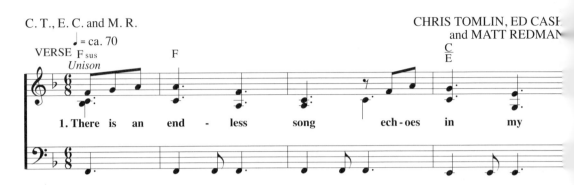

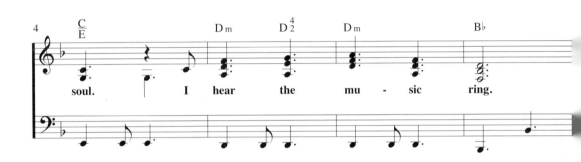

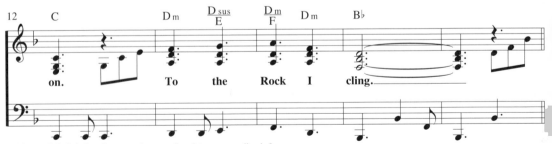

*This song is included on the companion recording. Intro on recording is 8 measures.

heart,— I am loved—— by the King, And it makes my heart— want to

sing.————

Grace Alone

39

Ephesians 2:4-9

S. W. B. and J. N.

♩ = ca. 80

SCOTT WESLEY BROWN
and JEFF NELSON

VERSES
Parts

1. Ev - 'ry prom - ise we can make, Ev - 'ry prayer and step of faith,
2. Ev - 'ry soul we long to reach, Ev - 'ry heart we hope to teach,

Ev - 'ry dif - f'rence we will make, is on - ly by His
Ev - 'ry-where we share His peace, is on - ly by His

The Family Prayer Song

Joshua 24:15

M. C.

MORRIS CHAPMAN

41
Centuries*

A.S.

AARON STRUMPEL

*This song is included on the companion recording. Intro on recording is 4 measures.

42

Majestic*

L. B.

♩ = ca. 126

LINCOLN BREWSTER

*This song is included on the companion recording. Intro on recording is 8 measures.

43

Love the Lord*

L. B.   LINCOLN BREWSTER

*This song is included on the companion recording. Intro is 4 measures.

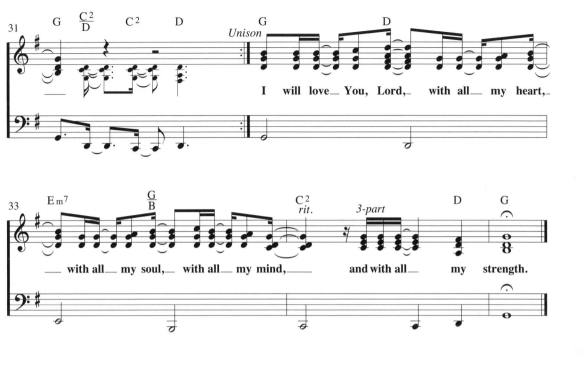

Thank You, Lord

44

Psalm 30:11-12

O. S.

OTIS SKILLINGS

Made to Worship*

45

E. C., C. T. and S. S.

ED CASH, CHRIS TOMLIN,
and STEPHAN SHARP

46

You Are Good

T. T.

TIM TIMMONS

47

O Praise Him*

DAVID CROWDER

*This song is included on the companion recording. Intro on recording is 4 measures.

48   Not to Us*

J. R. and C. T.   ♩ = ca. 112

JESSE REEVES and
CHRIS TOMLIN

1. The cross____ be - fore____ me, the world____ be - hind,____
2. Our hearts____ un - fold   be - fore____ Your_ throne,_

No turn - ing____ back,   raise the ban - ner____ high.
The on - ly____ place   for those____ who____ know.

cued note 1st time

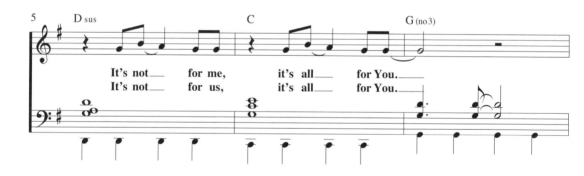

It's not____ for me,   it's all____ for You.____
It's not____ for us,   it's all____ for You.____

Let the heav - ens____ shake
Send Your ho - ly____ fire

*This song is included on the companion recording. Intro on recording is 12 measures.

spin - ning___ and sing - ing,_____ it's all for You.___ Your

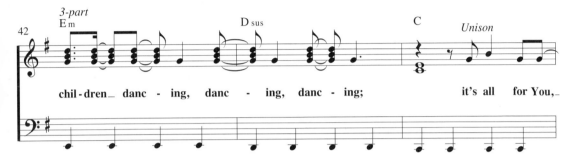

3-part

chil - dren___ danc - ing, danc - ing, danc - ing; it's all for You,_

it's all___ for You.___

Grace like Rain*

49

T. A. and C. C.

TODD AGNEW and
CHRIS COLLINS

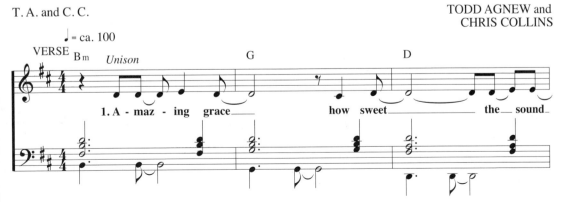

♩ = ca. 100

VERSE

1. A - maz - ing grace___ how sweet_____ the___ sound___

*This song is included on the companion recording. Intro on recording is 4 measures.

50

Alive Forever Amen

D. M., S. C. S and T. C.

DAVID MOFFITT, SUE C. SMITH
and TRAVIS COTTRELL

1. Let the chil - dren sing a song of lib - er - a - tion;
2. Let my heart sing out for Christ, the One and on - ly,

The God of our sal - va - tion set us free.
So pow - er - ful and ho - ly, res - cued me.

Death, where is thy sting? The curse of sin is bro - ken,
Death won't hurt me now be - cause He has re - deemed me,

The emp - ty tomb stands o - pen, come and see. He's a - live,
No grave will ev - er keep me from my King. I'm a - live,

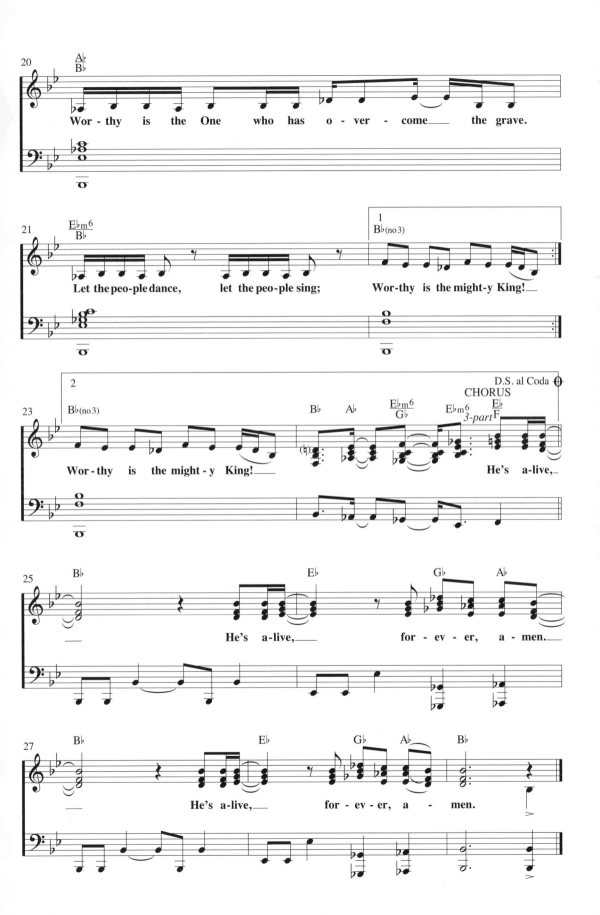

51 Let the Praises Ring*

L. B.

LINCOLN BREWSTER

1. O Lord,— my God,— in You I put— my trust.—

O Lord,— my God,— in You I put— my hope.—

O Lord,— my God,— in You I put— my trust.—

O Lord,— my God,— in You I put— my hope.—

CHORUS

In You,— in You— I find— my peace.

*This song is included on the companion recording. Intro on recording is 8 measures.

Let the prais - es_ ring!_
Let the prais - es_ ring!_
Let the prais - es_ ring!_

Wonderful, Magnificent God

Isaiah 28:29

52

GLENN PACKIAM

At Your feet I bow;_

There is none like_ You;_

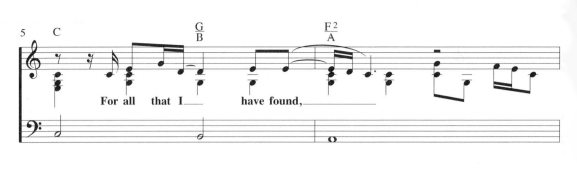

For all that I— have found,—————

All I want is— You;———

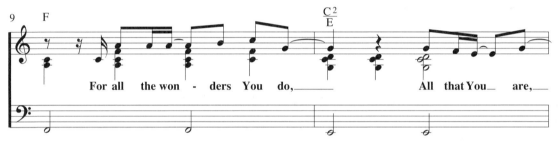

For all the won - ders You do,——— All that You— are,—

What can I— bring to You;—

— I of - fer my— heart.———

53 Revelation Song*

54 All the Earth Will Sing Your Praises

Our hearts are changed be-cause of
Your chil - dren stand to sing of

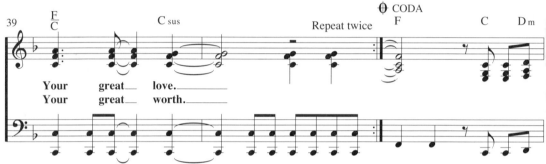

● CODA
Repeat twice   F

Your great__ love.__
Your great__ worth.__

All the earth__ will sing Your prais - es.__

55

I See You

Exodus 13:21-22

R. M.   RICH MULLINS
VERSES ♩ = ca. 75

1. Lord, You're lead - in' me (Lord, You're lead - in' me) with a cloud__
(2. And You take)__ my hand (And You take__ my hand) and You wash__

Here Is Our King*

56

DAVID CROWDER

*This song is included on the companion recording. Intro on recording is 4 measures.

57 Grace Flows Down*

2 Corinthians 8:9

L. G., R. P. and D. E. B.

LOUIE GIGLIO, ROD PADGETT
and DAVID E. BELL

*This song is included on the Volume 2 companion recording.

58 Your Grace Still Amazes Me

Ephesians 2:4-9

S. C. and C. H.

SHAWN CRAIG and
CONNIE HARRINGTON

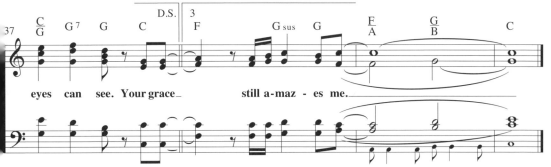

eyes can see. Your grace__ still a-maz - es me.__

Surrender

59

Philippians 3:7-14

1. I'm giv-ing You__ my heart, and all that is__ with-
2. I'm sing-ing You__ this song, I'm wait-ing at__ the__

in, I lay it all__ down for the sake of You,__ my
cross, And all the world__ holds dear, I count it all__ as

King; I'm giv-ing You__ my dreams, I'm lay - ing down my__ rights,
loss; For the sake of know - ing You, the glo - ry of__ Your__ name,__

Your Love Oh Lord*

60

B. A., D. C., M. P.,
M. L. and T. A.

BRAD AVERY, DAVID CARR,
MAC POWELL, MARK LEE
and TAI ANDERSON

*This song is included on the companion recording. Intro on recording is 8 measures.

61
Wonderful Maker*

M. R. and C. T.

MATT REDMAN and
CHRIS TOMLIN

Verse lyrics:

1. You spread out the skies o - ver emp - ty space Said, "Let there be light." In - to a dark and form - less world Your light was born.

(2.) eye has ful - ly seen, how beau - ti - ful the cross; And we have on - ly heard The faint - est whis - pers of how great You are.

PRE-CHORUS: You made the world and saw that it was good. You sent Your on - ly Son for You are____

62

Unchanging*

C. T.

CHRIS TOMLIN

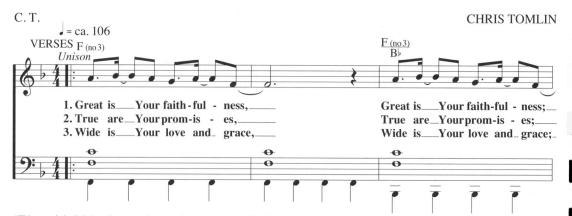

*This song is included on the companion recording. Intro on recording is 4 measures.

Rescue*

J. A.

JARED ANDERSON

64 Enthroned

have to wait to wor - ship for in our hearts You are en - throned.

Rock of Ages

Psalm 18:31

65

RITA BALOCHE

There is no Rock, there is no god___ like our___ God,___ No oth-er name___ wor - thy of all___ our praise.___

66 Word of God Speak*

B. M. and P. K.

BART MILLARD
and PETE KIPLEY

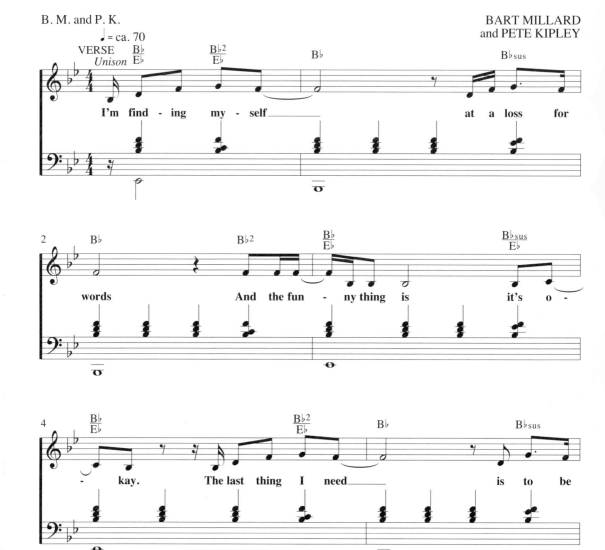

I'm find-ing my-self____ at a loss for words And the fun-ny thing is it's o-kay. The last thing I need____ is to be heard, But to hear____ what You would say.____

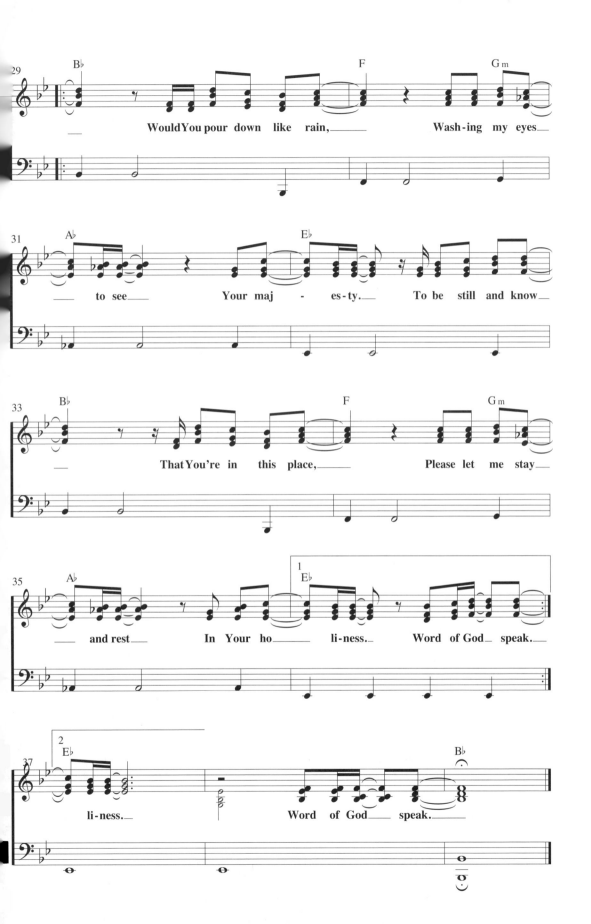

67
Every Road*

D. C.

DAVE CLARK

68

You're Everything*

C. B.   ♩ = ca. 83

CHRIS BARRON

*This song is included on the companion recording. Intro on recording is 4 measures.

CHORUS

To Save

came to seek___ and save___ the lost; He came to save,___ He

came to save._____ He came to give___ His life___ for us; He

came to seek___ and save___ the lost; He came to save,___ He

CHORUS
3-part

came to save.___ To save the world___ He gave___ His on - ly Son

___ So we could be-lieve_____ in Christ___ and

have e-ter - nal life._ He did-n't send_ His Son_ in-to_ the world

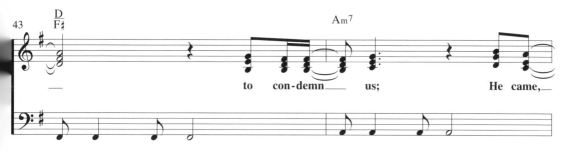

_ to con-demn _ us; He came,_

_ He came to save._

Take My Life*

70

FRANCES RIDLEY HAVERGAL,
CHRIS TOMLIN and LOUIE GIGLIO

HENRI A. CESAR MALAN,
CHRIS TOMLIN and LOUIE GIGLIO

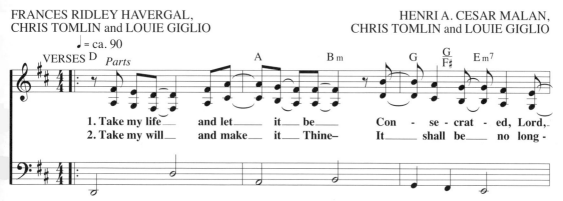

1. Take my life_ and let_ it be Con - se - crat - ed, Lord,_
2. Take my will_ and make_ it_ Thine– It_ shall be no long-

*This song is included on the companion recording. Intro on recording is 4 measures.

71 You're Worthy of My Praise*

Matthew 22:37-38

D.R.   ♩ = ca. 107

DAVID RUIS

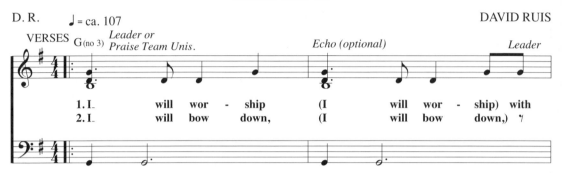

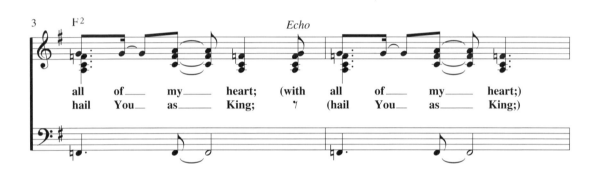

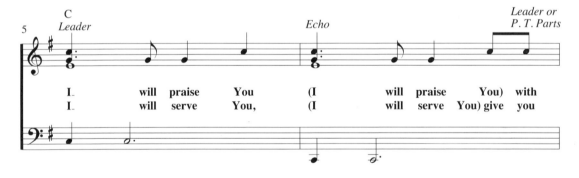

*This song is included on the companion recording. Intro on recording is 4 measures.
The recording and tracks have everyone singing the main parts in the verses.

Our God Saves*

72

P. B. and B. B.

PAUL BALOCHE and
BRENTON BROWN

*This song is included on the companion recording. Intro on the recording is 4 measures.

73
Never Will*

TIM TIMMONS

*This song is included on the companion recording. Intro on recording is 4 measures.

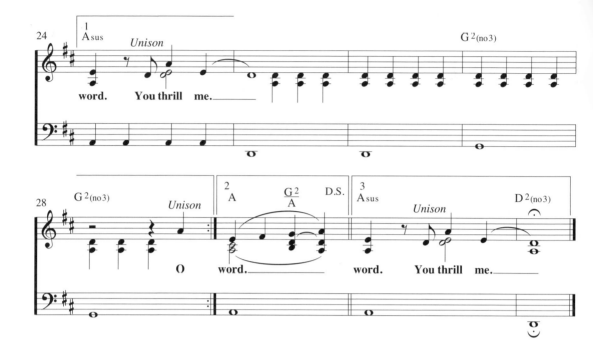

74   Everything Glorious*

*This song is included on the companion recording. Intro on recording is 8 measures.

75

He Will Rule the World

PHIL MEHRENS

P. M.

He will rule the world.___ He will rule the world.___

He will rule the world._____

Glory in the Highest*

76

C. T., J. R., E. C.,
D. C. and M. R.

CHRIS TOMLIN, JESSE REEVES,
ED CASH, DANIEL CARSON
and MATT REDMAN

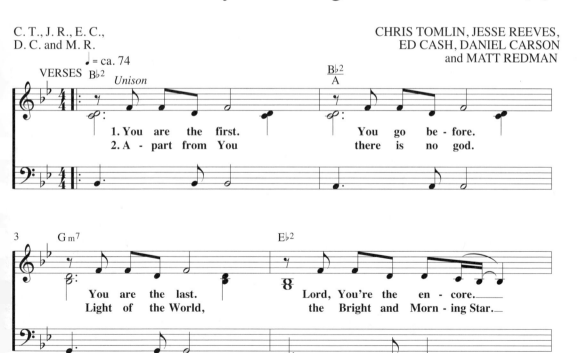

1. You are the first. You go be - fore.
2. A - part from You there is no god.

You are the last. Lord, You're the en - core.___
Light of the World, the Bright and Morn - ing Star.___

*This song is included on the companion recording. Intro on recording is 4 1/2 measures.

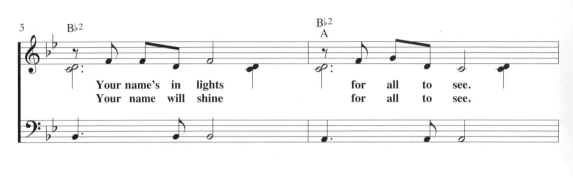

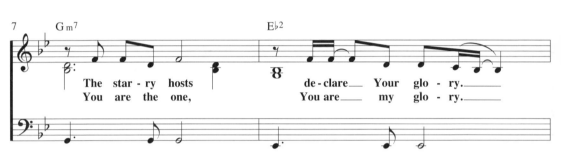

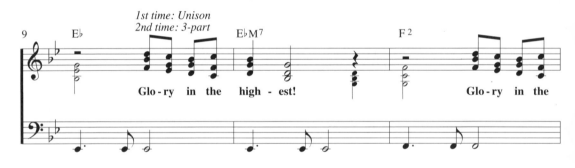

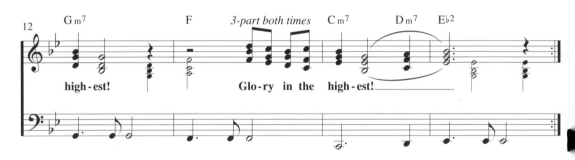

NOTE: The recording contains some altered base notes and chord progressions. The songbook matches the orchestration.

77   Center*

C. H. and M. R.

CHARLIE HALL
and MATT REDMAN

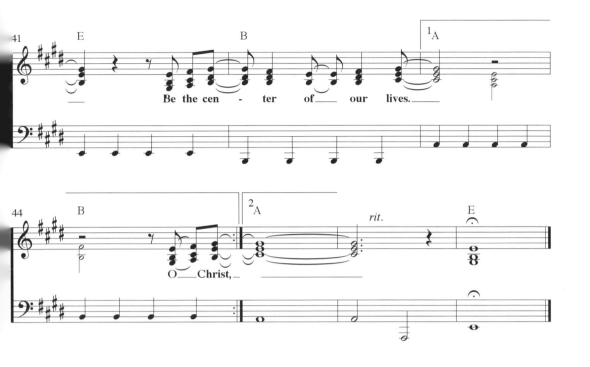

Here We Are*   **78**

CARTER ROBERTSON

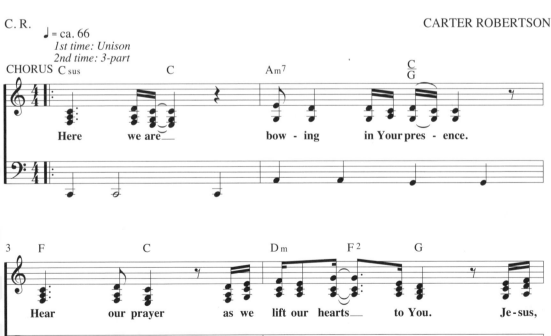

*This song is included on the companion recording. Intro on recording is 4 measures.

79 Give Me Your Hand*

Out - side His love!

80

Still

Psalm 46:10

REUBEN MORGAN

R. M. ♩ = ca. 72

1. Hide me now un - der Your wings.
(2.) rest my soul in Christ a - lone.

Cov - er me with -
Know His pow'r -

in Your might - y hand.
qui - et - ness and trust.

CHORUS 3-part

When the o - ceans

81

I See the Lord

Isaiah 6:1-3

CHRIS FALSON

82

God of Everything*

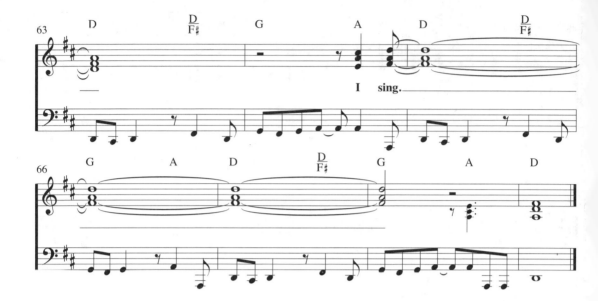

83

Holy Is the Lord*

Isaiah 6:3; Nehemiah 8:10

C. T. and L. G.

CHRIS TOMLIN and
LOUIE GIGLIO

We stand and lift up our hands, for the joy of the Lord is our strength. We bow down and wor - ship Him now; How great,

*This song is included on the companion recording. Intro on recording 4 measures.

*You may optionally omit measures 10-11 on 1st pass.

Turn Your Eyes upon Jesus

Hebrews 12:2

84

HELEN H. LEMMEL
and KEN BIBLE

HELEN H. LEMMEL

1. Turn your eyes up-on Je - sus, Look full in His won-der-ful face, And the things of earth will grow strange-ly dim, In the light of His glo - ry and grace.

2. Turn your eyes up-on Je - sus, Take hold of His pow-er-ful hand, He will lift you up in His might-y love, In the strength of your God you can stand.

85 Unfailing Love*

C. T., E. C. and C. P.

CHRIS TOMLIN, ED CASH
and CAREY PIERCE

VERSES ♩ = ca. 71

Unison

1. You have my heart, and I am Yours for -
(2. You are my) Rock, the One I hold on

ev - er; You are my strength, God of grace and
to; You are my song, and I sing for

pow - er. And ev - 'ry-thing You
You.

hold in Your hand. Still You make time for me, I can't

86 Glorious*

C. T. and J. R.

CHRIS TOMLIN
and JESSE REEVES

VERSES ♩ = ca. 96

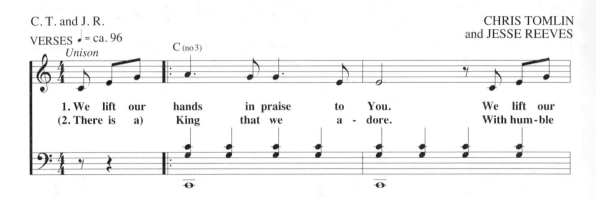

1. We lift our hands in praise to You. We lift our
(2. There is a) King that we a - dore. With hum - ble

hearts in wor - ship to You, Lord.
hearts we bow be - fore You, Lord.

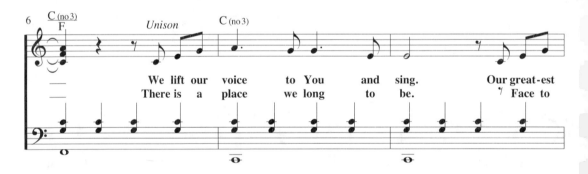

We lift our voice to You and sing. Our great-est
There is a place we long to be.   Face to

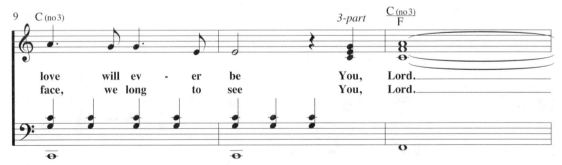

love will ev - er be You, Lord.
face, we long to see You, Lord.

*This song is included on the companion recording. Intro on recording is 4 measures.

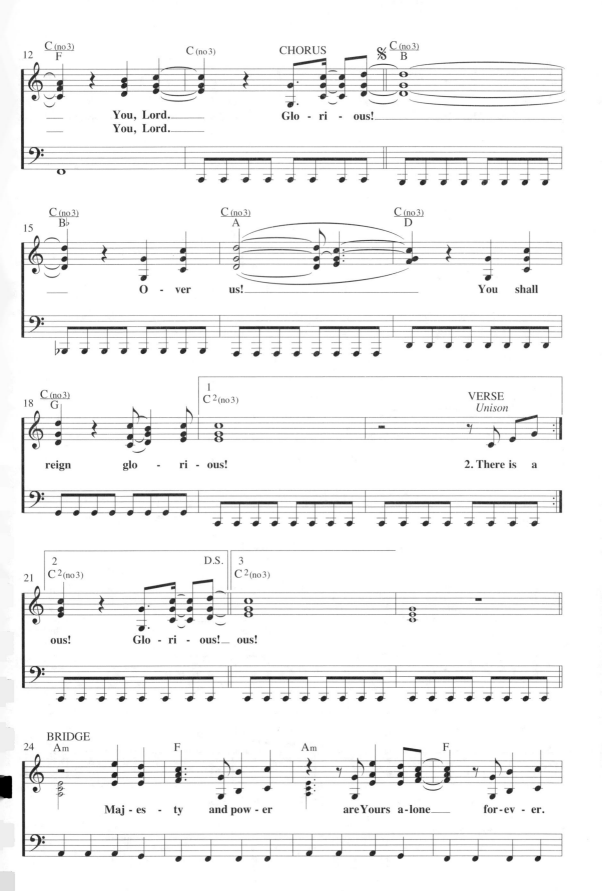

Lead Us On*

C. S.

CHRISTINE SCHMIDT

*This song is included on the companion recording. Intro on recording is 4 measures.

CHORUS

Find me o - pen,___ find me will - ing; I will walk___

___ this through___ with You.___

Find me here,___ all I am is all I'm bring - ing And I'll walk___

2nd time to Coda

___ this through___ with You.___

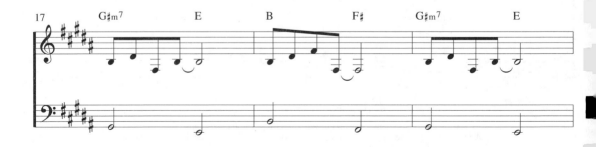

88 Sovereign Lord*

PHIL MEHRENS

*This song is included on the companion recording. Intro on recording is 4 measures.

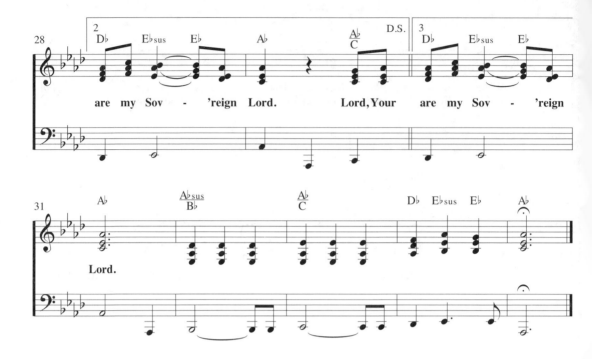

89 ## Lord, You Have My Heart

Psalm 108:1

MARTIN SMITH

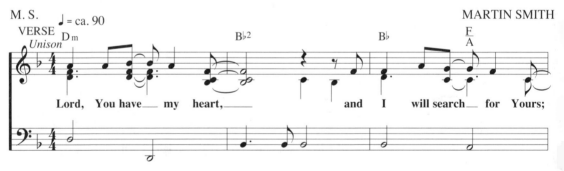

Lord, You have my heart, and I will search for Yours;

Je - sus, take my life and lead me

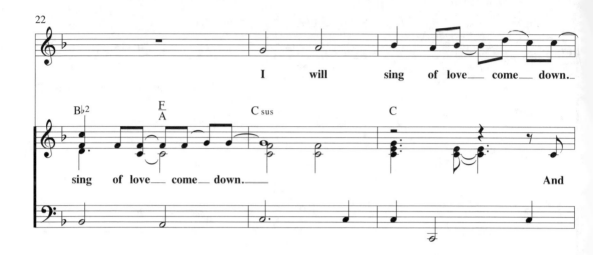

22

I will sing of love___ come___ down.

Bb2   F/A   C sus   C

sing   of love___ come___ down.___   And

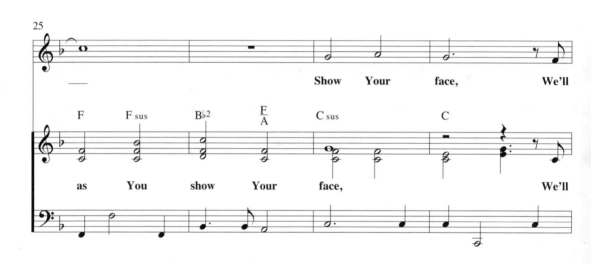

25

Show   Your   face,   We'll

F   F sus   Bb2   F/A   C sus   C

as   You   show   Your   face,   We'll

29

see   Your_____ glo - ry   here.

Bb   F/A   C sus   C   F   F sus   F

see   Your   glo - ry   here.

Lifesong*

M. H.

♩ = ca. 112

MARK HALL

VERSE (Unison)

1. Emp-ty hands held high, such small sac - ri - fice If not joined with my life, I sing in vain to - night.

PRE-CHORUS

May the words I say, and the things I do,

91   I Will Not Be Shaken*

*This song is included on the companion recording. Intro on recording is 4 measures.

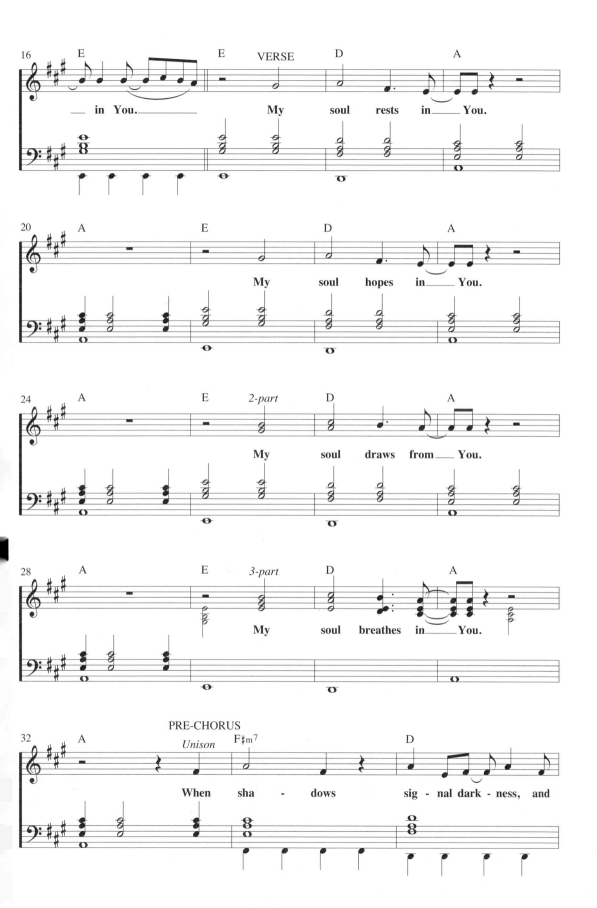

I will not___ be shak-en, no, I will not___ be moved;___ Though the o - cean swal-lows___ me, My heart's safe___ in You.___

92   Mighty Is the Power of the Cross*

S. C., C. T. and J. R.

SHAWN CRAIG, CHRIS TOMLIN and JESSE REEVES

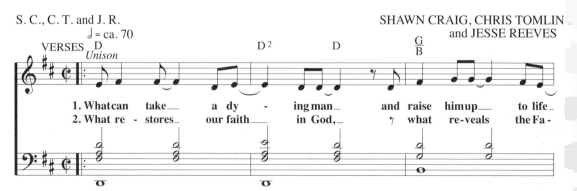

1. What can take___ a dy - ing man___ and raise him up___ to life___
2. What re - stores___ our faith___ in God,___ what re-veals the Fa -

*This song is included on the companion recording. Intro on recording is 8 measures.

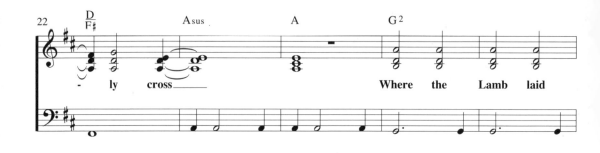

-ly cross_____ Where the Lamb laid

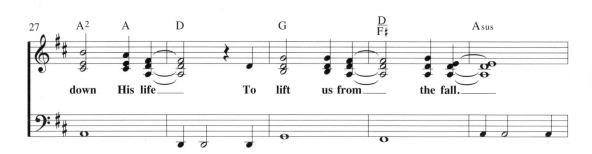

down His life_____ To lift us from_____ the fall._____

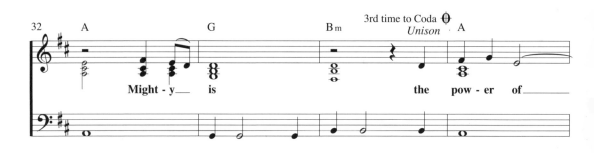

3rd time to Coda 🔵
Unison

Might - y___ is the pow - er of_____

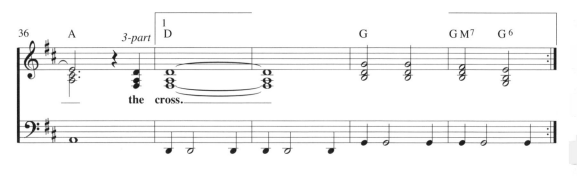

3-part

the cross._____

BRIDGE
Unison

cross. It's a mir - a - cle___ to me,_____ it's a

93 Your Name Is Holy

Luke 1:49

B. D.

BRIAN DOERKSEN

1. You are the sov - 'reign I Am. Your
2. You are the Al - might - y One. Your

name is ho - ly. You are the pure, spot - less
name is ho - ly. You are the Christ, God's own

Lamb. Your name is ho - ly.
Son. Your name is ho - ly.

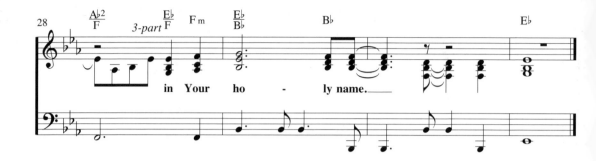

in Your ho - ly name.

94   Taste and See*

T. T.

TIM TIMMONS

Does an-y-bod-y here wan-na praise the Lord?

Yes, we'll praise the Lord. Does an-y-bod-y here wan-na

thank the Lord? Yes, we'll thank the Lord. He'll give His

*This song is included on the companion recording. Intro on recording is 4 measures.

95 Hope*

B. and C. R.

BARNY and CARTER ROBERTSON

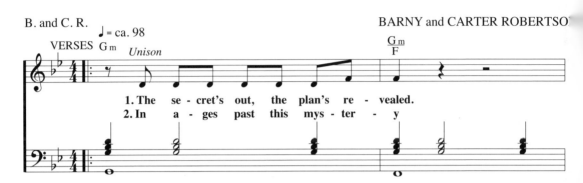

1. The se-cret's out, the plan's re-vealed.
2. In a-ges past this mys-ter-y

It's time to lis-ten to the truth.
Was hid-den in the great-er sto-ry.

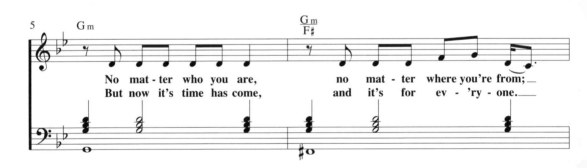

No mat-ter who you are, no mat-ter where you're from;
But now it's time has come, and it's for ev-'ry-one.

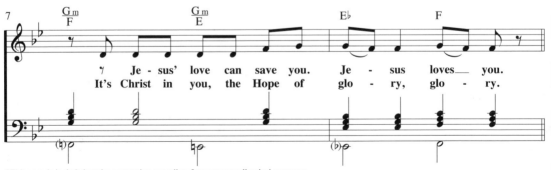

Je-sus' love can save you. Je-sus loves you.
It's Christ in you, the Hope of glo-ry, glo-ry.

*This song is included on the companion recording. Intro on recording is 4 measures.

96   How We Thank You*

T. T. and A. W.

TIM TIMMONS
and ADAM WATTS

*This song is included on the companion recording. Intro on recording is 4 measures.

We All Bow Down

Philippians 2:9-11

L.L.　♩ = ca. 74

LENNY LEBLANC

98

The Magnificat*

SHAWN GIESBRECHT

Lyrics:

O how I praise the Lord;

How I re-joice in God, my Sav-ior.

For He has filled my hun-gry heart;

He reached down and touched me.

*This song is included on the companion recording. Intro is 4 measures.

99 Carry Me

Exodus 19:4

K. H.
KYLE HILL

Car - ry me,___ Fa - ther God,___ on Your

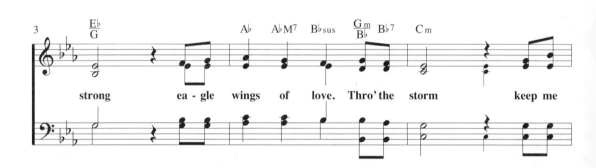

strong ea - gle wings of love. Thro' the storm keep me

safe; Thro' the tears and all my shame, car - ry me.___

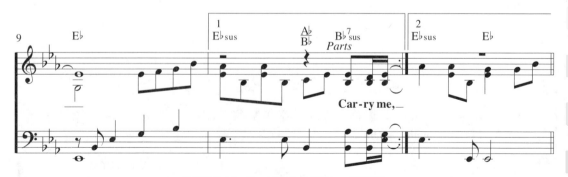

Car - ry me,___

100

The Power of the Cross*

S. T. and K. G.

STUART TOWNEND
and KEITH GETTY

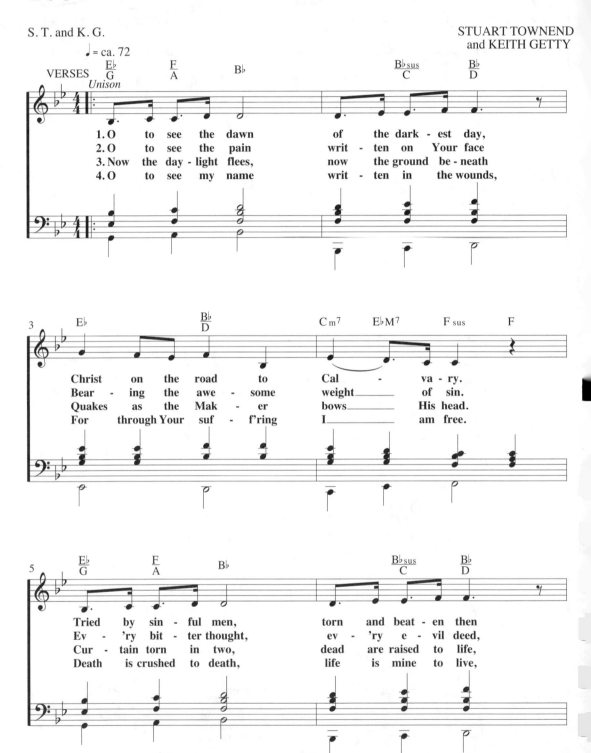

1. O to see the dawn of the dark - est day,
2. O to see the pain writ - ten on Your face
3. Now the day - light flees, now the ground be - neath
4. O to see my name writ - ten in the wounds,

Christ on the road to Cal - va - ry.
Bear - ing the awe - some weight_____ of sin.
Quakes as the Mak - er bows_____ His head.
For through Your suf - f'ring I_____ am free.

Tried by sin - ful men, torn and beat - en then
Ev - 'ry bit - ter thought, ev - 'ry e - vil deed,
Cur - tain torn in two, dead are raised to life,
Death is crushed to death, life is mine to live,

*This song is included on the companion recording. Intro on recording is 2 measures.

101 The Happy Song

Psalm 100:1-2

MARTIN SMITH

M. S.

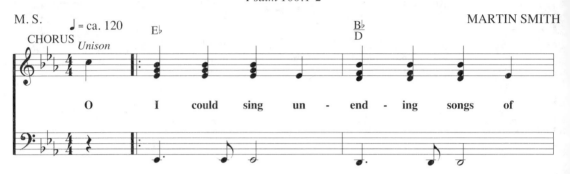

O I could sing un - end - ing songs of

how You saved my soul. Well, I could dance a

thou - sand miles be - cause of Your great love.

My heart is burst - ing, Lord, to tell of all___ You've done.

Index of Keys and Meter Signatures

*Songs marked with an asterisk (*)
are included on the companion recordings.

Topical Index with Keys

For a complete index of Scripture Backgrounds for each song, please visit the *All the Best Songs of Praise & Worship 3* product page at www.lillenas.com to download your free copy.

*Songs marked with an asterisk (*) are included on the companion recordings.

HYMNS

INVITATION

JESUS CHRIST—LORDSHIP

JESUS CHRIST—RESURRECTION

JESUS CHRIST—SUFFERING, DEATH & ATONEMENT

MAJESTY OF GOD

PALM SUNDAY

PRAISE & CELEBRATION

Alphabetical Index with Keys

*Songs marked with an asterisk (*)
are included on the companion recordings.